JERSEY

21 THINGS TO DO IN 7 DAYS

CW01460598

1. Mont Orgueil Castle

Mont Orgueil Castle, an iconic fortress perched above the picturesque village of Gorey, is one of Jersey's most celebrated landmarks. Overlooking the Royal Bay of Grouville, this castle has stood guard for more than 800 years, offering a fascinating glimpse into the island's history. Visitors can explore its labyrinth of staircases, secret rooms, and breathtaking vantage points, each telling stories of medieval defenses and political intrigue. The castle also houses captivating art installations and exhibits that bring history to life.

Mont Orgueil is located in the east of Jersey, roughly a 20-minute drive from St. Helier. Public buses (route 1) connect St. Helier to Gorey, with stops conveniently close to the castle. Parking is available nearby for those driving.

Tickets can be purchased online or on arrival. Prices are approximately £13 for adults, £8.50 for children (aged 6-16), and free for children under 6. Family passes are available at discounted rates. It's advisable to check opening hours and seasonal pricing on the official Jersey Heritage website, as they may vary.

Visitors should allocate at least 2-3 hours to fully appreciate Mont Orgueil Castle. Upon entry, a self-guided tour map is provided, and information panels throughout the castle explain its rich history. Highlights include the medieval Great Hall, the tower with panoramic views of the bay, and the "Dance of Death" artwork symbolizing the fragile nature of life during the castle's heyday. The "Witch's Stone" and hidden cellars are intriguing spots not to miss.

Comfortable footwear is essential due to steep stairs and uneven surfaces. The castle is partially wheelchair accessible, with specific areas designed for easier navigation. Gorey village, just below the castle, offers charming cafés and restaurants for a post-visit meal or snack.

Mont Orgueil is a must-visit for history buffs, families, and anyone captivated by stunning coastal views. Its timeless charm makes it an unforgettable part of any Jersey itinerary. Be sure to bring a camera, as the views over the harbor and the coastline are truly spectacular, especially during sunrise or sunset.

2. Elizabeth Castle

Elizabeth Castle, a historic fortress located on a tidal islet in St. Aubin's Bay, has been a significant defensive structure for over 300 years. Built during the reign of Queen Elizabeth I, it served as a key military stronghold and later as a residence for Governor Sir Walter Raleigh. Today, the castle offers a fascinating journey through Jersey's history, with exhibitions, military artifacts, and panoramic views of the bay. Accessible only at low tide or by ferry, it provides a unique experience for visitors.

The castle can be reached via the Castle Ferry, which departs from the slipway near St. Helier's Waterfront. During low tide, adventurous visitors can also walk across the causeway to the island. The ferry operates regularly during the day, with schedules dependent on the tides, and walking across requires sturdy footwear and caution.

Tickets for Elizabeth Castle cost approximately £13.40 for adults, £8.80 for children aged 6-16, and are free for children under 6. Family tickets and annual passes to multiple Jersey Heritage sites are also available. The ferry ride is an additional charge, around £3 for a return trip. It's recommended to check the Jersey Heritage website for up-to-date pricing and tide timings. Visitors should plan to spend 2-3 hours exploring the castle. Highlights include the Governor's House, the Hermitage where St. Helier, the island's patron saint, is said to have lived, and the bunkers used during World War II. The living history displays, including cannon firing and soldier reenactments, provide a vivid glimpse into the past. The views from the castle ramparts are breathtaking, showcasing the coastline and St. Helier's harbor.

Facilities include a café and picnic areas where visitors can relax while enjoying the scenic surroundings. The site has partial wheelchair accessibility, but steep steps and uneven paths in some areas make comfortable footwear essential. The ferry staff and visitor center provide maps and helpful guidance to ensure a smooth visit.

Elizabeth Castle is an unforgettable destination for history lovers, families, and those seeking spectacular coastal scenery. Whether exploring its fascinating exhibits or enjoying a tranquil moment overlooking the sea, the castle offers an enriching and memorable experience for all.

3. Jersey War Tunnels

The Jersey War Tunnels, originally known as Höhlgangsanlage 8, are a sprawling underground complex built by forced labor during the German occupation of Jersey in World War II. These tunnels served as a command center, barracks, and hospital for the German forces, and today, they stand as a moving memorial to the island's wartime experiences. Through interactive displays and powerful exhibits, visitors can learn about the occupation, resistance efforts, and the resilience of the islanders during this dark chapter in history.

Located in the parish of St. Lawrence, the Jersey War Tunnels are easily accessible by car or public transport. If driving, follow signs from St. Helier, approximately a 10-minute journey. Free parking is available on-site. Bus route 8 from Liberation Station in St. Helier also provides convenient access to the site.

Tickets cost around £15 for adults, £10 for children aged 7-16, and free for those under 7. Family tickets and annual passes are also available, offering good value for repeat visits or larger groups. It is recommended to purchase tickets in advance during peak seasons to avoid queues.

Visitors typically spend 2-3 hours exploring the tunnels. The site offers a self-guided tour with multilingual audio guides and detailed exhibits that chronicle the occupation period. Highlights include the Tunnel of Silence, which reflects on the forced laborers who built the tunnels, and the Liberation Room, commemorating Jersey's liberation in 1945. The authentic wartime artifacts, personal stories, and immersive settings provide a deeply emotional and educational experience.

The site has a café serving refreshments and a gift shop offering unique souvenirs. Comfortable footwear is advised as the tunnels are extensive, and the temperature remains cool throughout the year. The complex is partially wheelchair accessible, with assistance available for visitors requiring additional support.

The Jersey War Tunnels are a must-see for history enthusiasts and anyone interested in understanding the island's past. Offering a poignant look into the impact of war on Jersey's people, it is a place for reflection, learning, and honoring the resilience of those who lived through the occupation.

4. La Hougue Bie Museum

La Hougue Bie Museum is one of the oldest and most fascinating historical sites in Jersey, offering a glimpse into over 6,000 years of history. At its heart is a Neolithic passage grave, one of the largest and best-preserved examples in Europe. Visitors can explore the passage and chamber, marveling at its ancient construction. Above the mound sit two medieval chapels, adding layers of historical intrigue. The museum showcases artifacts unearthed at the site, alongside exhibitions about Jersey's archaeology and the story of the island through the ages. La Hougue Bie is located in the eastern part of the island, approximately a 15-minute drive from St. Helier. Public transport is available, with bus routes 3 and 13 stopping near the site. For those driving, parking is free and conveniently located.

Admission prices are around £10 for adults, £7 for children aged 6-16, and free for children under 6. Family tickets and discounted passes for multiple Jersey Heritage sites are also available. It's advisable to check the Jersey Heritage website for the latest opening times and seasonal prices.

Plan to spend 1.5-2 hours at La Hougue Bie Museum. Start with the main passage grave, which offers a rare opportunity to step inside a structure built over 6,000 years ago. The two chapels atop the mound provide stunning views of the surrounding countryside and a sense of the site's spiritual significance through time. The museum exhibits include fascinating archaeological finds such as tools, pottery, and the story of the treasure hoard discovered nearby. There's also an evocative memorial to slave workers who perished during the German occupation of Jersey, adding another layer of historical depth.

The site features a picnic area and a small café for refreshments. While the main museum and grounds are wheelchair accessible, access to the passage grave and chapels is limited due to steep and narrow paths. Comfortable shoes are recommended for exploring the mound and surrounding gardens.

La Hougue Bie Museum offers a unique journey through Jersey's history, combining ancient archaeology, medieval architecture, and poignant reminders of the past. Its tranquil setting and rich heritage make it a must-visit destination for those seeking a deeper connection with the island's history.

5. St. Brelade's Bay

St. Brelade's Bay is one of Jersey's most beautiful and popular beaches, known for its golden sands, calm waters, and stunning natural surroundings. Nestled on the island's southwestern coast, it is a perfect destination for relaxation, watersports, and family-friendly activities. The bay is bordered by picturesque gardens, a variety of cafés and restaurants, and the historic St. Brelade's Parish Church, which adds charm to its already idyllic setting. Its sheltered position makes it an ideal spot for swimming, paddleboarding, or simply enjoying a peaceful day by the sea.

Getting to St. Brelade's Bay is straightforward, with ample parking available nearby for those driving from St. Helier, which is about a 15-minute journey. Public buses (routes 12 and 14) also provide convenient access from various points on the island, with stops close to the beach.
The bay is free to visit, making it a cost-effective way to enjoy Jersey's stunning natural beauty. For those interested in watersports, equipment rentals for kayaking, paddleboarding, and windsurfing are available along the beach, with prices depending on the activity and duration. Sun loungers and parasols can also be rented for added comfort.

Visitors can easily spend a half or full day at St. Brelade's Bay. Activities include beachcombing, swimming, and exploring the nearby gardens and cliffside paths. A visit to St. Brelade's Parish Church and its adjacent Fisherman's Chapel is highly recommended, as both offer a glimpse into Jersey's religious and maritime history. The beach's promenade is lined with cafés, ice cream parlors, and restaurants serving fresh local seafood and international cuisine, perfect for a leisurely lunch or evening meal. While you're there, don't miss a chance to visit the beautiful L'Horizon Hotel, an iconic seaside retreat offering stunning views, luxury spa facilities, and exquisite dining options that elevate your beachside experience.

For families, the calm waters and soft sands provide a safe and enjoyable environment for children to play. Couples and solo travelers will appreciate the tranquil atmosphere and scenic views, especially during sunrise or sunset. Accessible facilities, including ramps and pathways, make the beach accommodating for all visitors.

St. Brelade's Bay offers something for everyone, combining natural beauty with opportunities for adventure and relaxation. Whether you're seeking a fun-filled day with the family or a peaceful retreat, this picturesque bay is a must-visit destination in Jersey.

6. Plemont Bay

Plemont Bay, located on Jersey's rugged northwestern coast, is a secluded haven known for its dramatic cliffs, golden sands, and fascinating caves. This hidden gem is a favorite among nature lovers and those seeking tranquility away from busier tourist spots. Accessible only at low tide, the beach reveals rock pools, waterfalls, and sea caves waiting to be explored, making it a unique destination for adventurers and families alike. Its unspoiled beauty and peaceful atmosphere make Plemont Bay a must-visit for anyone traveling to Jersey.

Getting to Plemont Bay requires a scenic drive, approximately 20 minutes from St. Helier. Parking is available at the clifftop, and a well-maintained but steep path leads down to the beach. Public transportation is limited, but bus route 8 connects to the area with a short walk from the nearest stop. Due to the tide's schedule, it's essential to plan your visit carefully to ensure enough time to explore the beach and safely return.

There is no entrance fee, making Plemont Bay an affordable and rewarding experience. Visitors should allocate at least 2-3 hours to enjoy the area fully. During low tide, you can explore the beach's fascinating caves, which are home to unique marine life. Children will love discovering creatures in the rock pools, while the expansive sands are perfect for sunbathing or a picnic. The surrounding cliffs provide excellent vantage points for photography and birdwatching, with species such as puffins and kestrels often spotted in the area.

The beach itself has no facilities, but the nearby Plemont Bay Café offers refreshments, snacks, and breathtaking views of the bay. Comfortable walking shoes are recommended due to the steep access path, and visitors should bring their own supplies, including water and towels, for a more enjoyable outing.

Plemont Bay is best suited for those who appreciate nature's raw beauty and are comfortable navigating its remote terrain. Its serene environment and stunning scenery make it a perfect spot for unwinding, exploring, or simply soaking in the beauty of Jersey's coastline. For a truly magical experience, time your visit during the late afternoon and watch the sunset cast a golden glow over the bay.

7. Jersey Zoo (Durrell Wildlife Park)

Jersey Zoo, also known as Durrell Wildlife Park, is a world-renowned conservation center founded by Gerald Durrell in 1959. Nestled in the lush countryside of Trinity Parish, the zoo is dedicated to saving species from extinction and is home to a wide variety of rare and endangered animals. Visitors can encounter gorillas, orangutans, lemurs, and reptiles, as well as learn about the zoo's global conservation efforts. With its beautifully landscaped grounds and focus on education and sustainability, Jersey Zoo offers a unique and inspiring experience for all ages.

The zoo is approximately a 15-minute drive from St. Helier, with ample parking available on-site. Public buses, such as route 3, provide easy access to the zoo, with regular departures from Liberation Station. For those cycling, bike racks are available at the entrance, making it a convenient and eco-friendly option.

Tickets cost approximately £17 for adults and £13 for children aged 4-16, with free entry for children under 4. Family passes and annual memberships are also available, offering great value for larger groups or frequent visitors. It is recommended to book tickets online in advance, especially during busy periods, to ensure availability and save time.

Plan to spend 3-4 hours at Jersey Zoo to fully explore its exhibits and grounds. Highlights include the Gorilla Enclosure, the Butterfly House, and the Reptile Amphibian Center, which showcases rare species such as the endangered ploughshare tortoise. The Lemur Walkthrough offers a close-up encounter with these playful creatures, while the fruit bat exhibit is a favorite for its immersive design. Guided tours, talks, and feeding sessions provide further insights into the zoo's conservation work and its residents.

On-site facilities include a café serving locally sourced food, a picnic area, and a gift shop with souvenirs supporting the zoo's mission. The grounds are wheelchair accessible, with paths suitable for strollers and mobility aids. Comfortable footwear is recommended due to the size of the park, and there are plenty of shaded areas for rest breaks.

Jersey Zoo is an unmissable attraction for animal lovers and conservation enthusiasts. Combining fun, education, and a commitment to wildlife preservation, it offers a memorable day out that contributes to a vital cause. Be sure to bring a camera to capture the beautiful surroundings and incredible wildlife encounters.

8. Samares Manor

Samares Manor, located in the parish of St. Clément, is a historic estate that offers a tranquil retreat and a glimpse into Jersey's past. The manor house, dating back to the 12th century, was once the home of several notable families, and today it is open to the public as a museum and heritage site. The estate is renowned for its beautiful gardens, which include a walled garden, an impressive orchard, and a well-maintained kitchen garden. The manor is an excellent destination for history enthusiasts, gardeners, and those looking for a peaceful escape in a scenic setting.

Samares Manor is easily accessible by car, located about 10 minutes from St. Helier. There is ample free parking on-site for visitors. If you are using public transportation, bus routes 1, 15, and 22 stop nearby, and it is a short walk from the bus stop to the entrance.

Tickets to Samares Manor are approximately £10 for adults, £6 for children aged 5-16, and free for children under 5. Family tickets and annual passes are also available, providing great value for families or those planning multiple visits. The estate is open daily from 10 AM to 5 PM, but it's recommended to check the website for any seasonal changes or special events before your visit.

Visitors typically spend 1.5 to 2 hours exploring Samares Manor. Begin with a stroll around the meticulously designed gardens, which include a variety of flowers, herbs, and shrubs. The walled garden offers a beautiful space for quiet reflection, while the orchard displays fruit trees typical of the island's agricultural heritage. The kitchen garden showcases the manor's historical connection to food production, with vegetables grown as they would have been in centuries past.

Inside the manor house, you can explore the rooms that display artifacts from its storied past, including furniture, paintings, and documents. The manor also offers information on its role in Jersey's history, including its connection to the island's aristocratic families. The on-site café serves refreshments, making it a great spot to relax after your tour.

Samares Manor is a peaceful and educational destination, offering an insight into Jersey's history and horticultural traditions. Whether you're interested in the history of the manor, the stunning gardens, or simply enjoying a leisurely walk, it is a wonderful place to explore.

9. Gorey Village

Gorey Village, located on the eastern coast of Jersey, is a charming and historic destination with a delightful blend of old-world character and scenic beauty. The village is best known for its stunning views of the sea, the imposing Gorey Castle, and its cobbled streets lined with quaint shops, cafes, and restaurants. A visit to Gorey offers a chance to experience Jersey's rich maritime history, as well as its vibrant local culture. The village is a peaceful yet lively place, perfect for those looking to explore Jersey's coastal heritage while enjoying a relaxed atmosphere.

Gorey Village is easily accessible from St. Helier, just a 15-minute drive away. There is plenty of parking available in the village, and the area is also well-served by public transport, with regular bus routes connecting it to the island's capital. For those arriving by bicycle, bike racks are available, and the village's scenic streets make it a pleasant spot for cyclists.

There is no admission fee to explore the village itself, and visitors can enjoy wandering through the narrow streets and taking in the picturesque surroundings for free. For those interested in the castle, the entrance fee to Gorey Castle is around £10 for adults and £7 for children, with discounts for families and annual passes available. The castle is open daily, but it's a good idea to check the schedule for guided tours or special events, which often provide deeper insight into its history.

Exploring Gorey Village typically takes around 2-3 hours. Start with a visit to Gorey Castle, where you can learn about its history and enjoy panoramic views of the island. From there, take a leisurely stroll along the harbor, where you'll find small shops offering local products and seafood. The area is perfect for a relaxed lunch, with various cafes offering freshly prepared meals and local delicacies. Don't forget to visit the Fishermen's Chapel, which adds to the village's historic charm.

Gorey is also home to several small art galleries and boutique shops, making it an ideal place to pick up souvenirs or enjoy local craftsmanship. Whether you are taking in the views, savoring local food, or exploring the village's history, Gorey offers a fulfilling and scenic experience perfect for a half-day visit.

10. St. Helier Marina

St. Helier Marina is a bustling harbor located in the heart of Jersey's capital, offering a lively mix of maritime activity, shopping, dining, and scenic views. The marina serves as a base for yachts, boats, and ferries and is one of the island's most picturesque locations, providing an excellent spot to explore Jersey's maritime heritage while enjoying a leisurely day by the sea. With its proximity to the town center, St. Helier Marina is a convenient starting point for visitors looking to experience both the island's natural beauty and vibrant city life.

St. Helier Marina is easily accessible, located within walking distance of St. Helier's main shopping area. If arriving by car, there are several nearby car parks, including a multi-story car park just a short walk from the marina. Alternatively, buses from various parts of the island regularly stop near the marina, making public transport a convenient option for getting there.

There is no entry fee to visit St. Helier Marina itself, so visitors can freely explore the area, stroll along the waterfront, or relax at one of the many benches along the quayside. The marina is also home to a number of shops, cafes, and restaurants offering both local and international cuisine, ideal for a leisurely lunch or dinner. For those interested in water-based activities, boat tours, sailing trips, and ferry rides to nearby islands can be booked at the marina. Prices for these activities vary depending on the tour or service, with typical boat tours starting around £20 per person.

Visitors typically spend between 1.5 to 2 hours at the marina, depending on how much time they wish to spend enjoying the scenery or dining. One of the highlights of a visit is a walk along the harbor, where you can admire the colorful yachts and boats and watch the bustling marine life. For those interested in Jersey's maritime history, nearby attractions such as the Maritime Museum are just a short walk away, providing further insights into the island's seafaring past. St. Helier Marina is a great spot for both relaxation and exploration, offering something for everyone. Whether you're enjoying the vibrant atmosphere, taking a boat trip, or simply watching the world go by, the marina provides a picturesque setting for a memorable visit.

11. The Waterfront at St. Helier

The Waterfront at St. Helier is a vibrant and picturesque area located along the waterfront of Jersey's capital, offering a blend of shopping, dining, cultural attractions, and scenic views. This modern development is a focal point for visitors looking to enjoy the best of both local and international offerings while taking in the beauty of the harbor. Whether you're interested in leisurely walks along the quayside, exploring local art, or dining at waterfront cafes, the Waterfront provides a perfect setting for a relaxed yet engaging day out.

Getting to the Waterfront is easy from St. Helier's town center, located just a short walk away. It's well-served by public transport, with buses regularly stopping nearby. If you're driving, there are several parking options available, including a large parking facility near the waterfront, providing convenient access for visitors.

There is no entry fee for visiting the Waterfront area, and visitors are free to wander around the quayside, browse the shops, or enjoy a coffee with a view. The area is home to a wide range of restaurants, cafes, and bars, offering everything from local seafood to international cuisine. The waterfront is especially popular for casual dining, with many eateries offering outdoor seating, allowing guests to enjoy the beautiful harbor views. Visitors can also take advantage of nearby food markets and festivals, which often feature local produce and Jersey delicacies.

A visit to the Waterfront typically takes around 2 hours, depending on your interests. For those interested in culture, the nearby Jersey Museum & Art Gallery offers an in-depth look into the island's history and art scene, and is within walking distance of the Waterfront. The museum has an entrance fee, typically around £10 for adults and £5 for children. Additionally, visitors can take a scenic walk along the marina or enjoy the stunning views of Elizabeth Castle, which can be easily accessed via boat trips that depart from the Waterfront.

The Waterfront is also a prime location for enjoying water-based activities such as kayaking or paddleboarding, which can be rented nearby. Whether you're relaxing by the water, exploring the shops, or enjoying a meal with a view, the Waterfront at St. Helier offers a refreshing and enjoyable experience, ideal for those wanting to experience Jersey's lively coastal atmosphere.

12. Corbière Lighthouse

Corbière Lighthouse, located at the southwestern tip of Jersey, is one of the island's most iconic landmarks. This majestic lighthouse, which has been guiding ships safely for over 150 years, stands proudly at the edge of the rugged coastline, offering breathtaking views of the Atlantic Ocean and the surrounding cliffs. The lighthouse is accessible by foot, car, or bus, making it an easy and rewarding destination for visitors to Jersey who want to experience its natural beauty and maritime heritage.

To get to Corbière Lighthouse, it's a scenic 20-minute drive from St. Helier, with plenty of parking available nearby. The lighthouse is also accessible via bus routes 1 and 15, which run regularly from St. Helier and other parts of the island. Visitors can also choose to cycle or walk to the lighthouse along the coastal path, which provides stunning views of the shoreline and surrounding landscape. The walk from the nearby Corbière car park to the lighthouse takes around 5-10 minutes, making it a quick and easy visit.

There is no admission fee to visit Corbière Lighthouse itself, but visitors can enjoy the surrounding area, including the rocky beaches and tide pools, for free. If you're interested in learning more about the lighthouse and its history, you can visit the nearby visitor center, where you can find information on the history of the lighthouse, the island's maritime tradition, and the surrounding coastal wildlife.

The area around Corbière Lighthouse is perfect for a leisurely exploration, with a variety of activities available for nature lovers and photographers. Spend some time walking along the cliff paths, taking in the stunning panoramic views, or simply relaxing by the sea. The lighthouse is particularly striking during sunset, when the light casts a golden glow over the surrounding coastline. If you're visiting during low tide, explore the nearby rock pools, which are home to a range of marine life.

A visit to Corbière Lighthouse typically takes 1.5 to 2 hours, depending on how long you wish to spend enjoying the views and exploring the area. Don't forget to bring your camera, as the lighthouse and its surroundings offer plenty of opportunities for stunning photos. Whether you're interested in the history, the natural beauty, or simply enjoying a peaceful coastal walk, Corbière Lighthouse is a must-visit destination during your trip to Jersey.

13. Jersey Museum and Art Gallery

The Jersey Museum and Art Gallery, located in the heart of St. Helier, is a must-visit destination for those interested in learning about the island's rich history and vibrant art scene. The museum offers a fascinating insight into Jersey's cultural heritage, showcasing a wide range of exhibits, from archaeological finds to contemporary art. Housed in a beautifully restored Georgian building, the museum also offers a variety of interactive displays and educational programs, making it a great place for both adults and families.

To get to the museum, it's just a short walk from the main shopping area in St. Helier. The museum is centrally located and is easily accessible by foot, car, or public transport. If you're driving, there are several car parks nearby, including one at the Liberation Station, just a few minutes' walk away. The museum is also well-served by bus routes, making it convenient to reach from other parts of the island.

The entrance fee to the museum is around £10 for adults, £5 for children, and there are discounted family tickets available. For those who wish to explore more of Jersey's history, the museum offers combined tickets for entry to other nearby attractions, such as the Maritime Museum, at a reduced price. The museum is open daily from 10 AM to 5 PM, though it's always a good idea to check ahead for any special events or closures, especially during the off-season. A visit to the Jersey Museum and Art Gallery typically takes around 1.5 to 2 hours.

The museum's exhibitions are spread over several floors, so there's plenty to explore. The museum's history section focuses on Jersey's development over the centuries, from prehistoric times to the modern day, with displays covering topics such as the island's role in the Napoleonic Wars, its agricultural heritage, and its industrial past. The art gallery showcases a range of works by both local and international artists, with a special focus on the work of Jersey artists throughout history.

The museum also offers a café where visitors can relax and enjoy a light meal or a coffee, making it a great place to unwind after exploring the exhibits. For those looking for unique souvenirs, the museum shop offers a selection of locally made crafts, books, and art prints. Whether you're interested in Jersey's past or its contemporary art scene, the Jersey Museum and Art Gallery offers a well-rounded and enriching experience.

14. The Orchid Foundation

The Orchid Foundation, located in the beautiful parish of St. Ouen, Jersey, is a peaceful and picturesque garden dedicated to the cultivation and conservation of orchids. This nonprofit organization offers visitors a unique opportunity to explore a wide variety of orchids in a stunning, natural setting. The foundation aims to educate the public about the importance of preserving orchid species and their role in biodiversity. The Orchid Foundation is home to a vast collection of orchids, including rare and endangered species, making it a must-visit for nature enthusiasts and plant lovers.

To get to The Orchid Foundation, it is best to drive from St. Helier, which takes about 20 minutes. There is parking available at the entrance, making it easy for visitors to access the gardens. Alternatively, public buses operate on a regular schedule, with routes connecting St. Helier to St. Ouen. The bus ride offers a scenic view of the island, and the stop is just a short walk from the garden's entrance.

The entry fee for The Orchid Foundation is modest, typically around £7 for adults and £3 for children. The foundation also offers discounted rates for groups and families, and sometimes special events are held at a higher ticket price. The garden is open to visitors from April to October, and it's advisable to check ahead for specific opening hours, especially during off-peak times or for any special events.

A visit to The Orchid Foundation usually takes about 1.5 to 2 hours. Upon arrival, guests are greeted by a lush and colorful landscape filled with a wide variety of orchids. The garden features both indoor and outdoor orchid displays, with tropical, temperate, and woodland species on display. Visitors can stroll through the peaceful grounds, learning about the different types of orchids and their growing conditions. The knowledgeable staff are happy to answer any questions and share insights into the conservation efforts taking place at the foundation.

In addition to exploring the orchid displays, visitors can visit the gift shop, which offers a range of orchid-related products, including plants, books, and unique handcrafted items. There is also a small café where guests can enjoy a coffee or light snack while taking in the beauty of the garden. Whether you are an orchid enthusiast or simply looking to enjoy a serene day in nature, The Orchid Foundation offers an enriching and relaxing experience on the island of Jersey.

15. Rozel Bay

Rozel Bay, located on the northeast coast of Jersey, is a charming and picturesque spot known for its natural beauty, calm waters, and tranquil atmosphere. This small, sheltered bay offers stunning views of the surrounding cliffs and is an ideal destination for visitors looking to escape the busier areas of the island. Whether you're seeking a relaxing day by the sea, a scenic walk, or a chance to enjoy local seafood, Rozel Bay has something to offer.

To get to Rozel Bay, it's a scenic drive of about 20 minutes from St. Helier. The bay is accessible by car, with ample parking available nearby. For those relying on public transport, bus routes 1, 2, and 3 regularly stop in the area, making it easy to reach from St. Helier and other parts of the island. Visitors can also enjoy the picturesque walk to the bay, as there are several coastal paths in the area that offer beautiful views of the surrounding landscape.

There is no entry fee for visiting Rozel Bay, so it's a free destination to enjoy. Many people come to relax on the beach, which is perfect for sunbathing, picnicking, and swimming in the calm waters. The bay is particularly popular with families, as its sheltered nature makes it a safe place for children to paddle and play. For those who enjoy a bit of history, the nearby Rozel Harbour, with its quaint cottages and small fishing boats, is a lovely place to explore.

Visitors can spend a few hours enjoying the bay, but there are also other activities in the area. The bay is home to a handful of excellent cafes and restaurants serving fresh local seafood and traditional Jersey dishes. Rozel Bay is particularly well-known for its seafood, and the popular Rozel Bay Café is an excellent spot for a leisurely lunch with a view of the water.

A visit to Rozel Bay typically takes between 1.5 to 3 hours, depending on how much time you spend enjoying the beach, exploring the surroundings, or dining. For those who enjoy coastal walks, there are several nearby trails that lead to scenic viewpoints, such as the cliff paths that connect Rozel Bay to the neighboring beaches and villages. With its serene atmosphere, stunning natural beauty, and opportunity for relaxation, Rozel Bay is a perfect getaway for anyone visiting Jersey.

16. Greve de Lecq Beach

Greve de Lecq Beach, located on the northern coast of Jersey, is one of the island's most popular and scenic beaches. This family-friendly beach is known for its golden sand, clear waters, and surrounding cliffs, making it a perfect spot for both relaxation and outdoor activities. Whether you're interested in swimming, sunbathing, or simply enjoying the stunning views, Greve de Lecq Beach offers something for everyone.

To get to Greve de Lecq Beach, it's about a 25-minute drive from St. Helier, the island's capital. There is ample parking available at the beach, though it can get busy during peak summer months. For those relying on public transport, buses 1, 15, and 16 serve the area and stop near the beach. Visitors can also explore the surrounding coastal paths, which offer scenic walks with breathtaking views of the shoreline.

There is no entry fee to visit Greve de Lecq Beach, making it a free destination for visitors. The beach is ideal for swimming, as the waters are generally calm and safe, with lifeguards present during the summer season. The sandy shore is perfect for sunbathing, picnicking, or simply relaxing with a good book. For those interested in water sports, the beach is also popular for kayaking, paddleboarding, and windsurfing. The surrounding rock pools offer great opportunities for exploring marine life at low tide, making it a fun activity for families and children.

Visitors can also enjoy a stroll along the beach to the nearby Greve de Lecq Barracks, a historic site that dates back to the 18th century. The barracks offer a glimpse into Jersey's military past and provide a fascinating look at how the island was defended during times of conflict. The nearby cliffs offer excellent opportunities for photography, as they provide panoramic views of the beach and the surrounding coastline.

There are several cafés and eateries located near the beach, where visitors can enjoy a light snack or a full meal with a view of the sea. The Greve de Lecq Café is a popular spot for fresh local seafood, sandwiches, and drinks. A visit to Greve de Lecq Beach typically takes around 2 to 3 hours, but visitors can easily spend longer enjoying the beach, exploring the surroundings, or dining at one of the local restaurants. With its natural beauty and variety of activities, Greve de Lecq Beach is a must-see destination for anyone visiting Jersey.

17. Beauport Beach

Beauport Beach, located on the southern coast of Jersey, is one of the island's hidden gems, offering a serene and secluded escape. Known for its stunning natural beauty, this small but picturesque bay is surrounded by rugged cliffs, lush greenery, and clear blue waters, making it a perfect spot for those looking to enjoy Jersey's coastline in a more tranquil setting. The beach is ideal for swimming, sunbathing, or simply enjoying a peaceful day by the sea.

To reach Beauport Beach, visitors can drive from St. Helier, which takes about 15 minutes. The beach is accessible via a steep, narrow path that descends from the cliff top, so be prepared for a bit of a walk, though the stunning views make the effort well worth it. There is limited parking at the top of the hill, so it's recommended to arrive early during peak seasons to secure a spot. Alternatively, public buses can get you close to the beach, with a short walk from the nearest bus stop.

There is no entry fee to visit Beauport Beach, making it an excellent free destination for visitors. While the beach is relatively small, it is known for its sheltered location, which makes the waters calm and inviting, perfect for a refreshing swim or a paddle in the clear blue sea. The beach is not as crowded as some of Jersey's more popular beaches, so visitors can often find a peaceful spot to relax or sunbathe. The surrounding cliffs provide an excellent backdrop for photos, and the area is also a great spot for birdwatching and enjoying Jersey's natural environment.

For those interested in exploring the area further, Beauport Beach is surrounded by scenic coastal paths that offer stunning views of the island's shoreline and nearby beaches. The nearby headlands also provide excellent opportunities for walking and photography, with the paths leading to other hidden coves and beaches. The area is also home to a variety of local wildlife, and the calm waters make it an ideal location for kayaking and paddleboarding.

Visitors typically spend around 1.5 to 2 hours at Beauport Beach, although those who enjoy hiking or exploring the surrounding area may want to stay longer. While there are no facilities directly on the beach, nearby restaurants and cafes in the surrounding area offer light refreshments. For a peaceful and picturesque day by the sea, Beauport Beach is an ideal choice for those visiting Jersey.

18. The Living Legend Village

The Living Legend Village, located in the heart of Jersey, offers visitors a unique and immersive experience into the island's rich history and folklore. This interactive attraction brings Jersey's legends, myths, and historic events to life through a series of engaging displays and reenactments. The village is designed to offer a fun and educational experience for visitors of all ages, making it an ideal destination for families, history enthusiasts, and anyone interested in learning more about the island's cultural heritage.

To reach The Living Legend Village, it is a short drive from St. Helier, taking approximately 15 minutes. The village is located in a rural setting, so driving is the most convenient way to get there. There is ample parking available on-site for visitors. For those using public transport, buses regularly run from St. Helier to nearby stops, with a short walk from the bus stop to the village. The village is open year-round, but it's best to check the schedule for specific opening times and any seasonal events.

The entry fee for The Living Legend Village is typically around £10 for adults and £6 for children, with discounts available for families and groups. Tickets can be purchased on-site or in advance through the village's website. The attraction is open from April to October, and it's worth noting that special events or themed days may require advanced booking.

Visitors to The Living Legend Village can explore various exhibits that delve into Jersey's ancient and medieval past, with a focus on local legends such as the stories of mythical creatures and historical figures. The village features life-size models and immersive displays that recreate scenes from Jersey's history, including its Viking and Norman past. Interactive elements allow guests to participate in the storytelling, from dressing up as historical figures to engaging in hands-on activities.

A visit typically takes around 1.5 to 2 hours, depending on how much time you spend exploring the exhibits. There are guided tours available, which can enrich your experience with deeper insights into Jersey's folklore. The village also has a café where visitors can enjoy light refreshments and take a break while absorbing the historical atmosphere. The Living Legend Village is not just about history—it's a celebration of Jersey's unique cultural heritage, making it a must-see for anyone visiting the island looking for an engaging and memorable experience.

19. Bonne Nuit Bay

Bonne Nuit Bay, located on the northern coast of Jersey, is a peaceful and scenic spot offering visitors a serene retreat away from the island's more bustling areas. The bay is known for its sheltered location, rocky shores, and beautiful views, making it a popular destination for those looking to enjoy Jersey's natural beauty. Whether you're looking to relax on the beach, explore the surrounding cliffs, or learn about the area's maritime history, Bonne Nuit Bay offers a range of activities for all types of visitors.

To get to Bonne Nuit Bay, it's about a 25-minute drive from St. Helier. The bay is accessible by car, with parking available nearby, although spaces can fill up quickly, especially during the summer months. If you are relying on public transport, buses 1 and 2 serve the area, though the journey requires a short walk from the bus stop to the bay. For those who enjoy hiking, the area is surrounded by several coastal paths, which provide stunning views of the shoreline and are ideal for a scenic walk to the bay.

There is no entry fee to visit Bonne Nuit Bay, making it a free and accessible destination. The bay is perfect for swimming, as the waters are generally calm and safe, ideal for families with children. The rocky shoreline is also great for those interested in exploring rock pools and observing local marine life at low tide. The area is known for its clear waters and excellent visibility, so snorkelers and divers often enjoy exploring the underwater world around the bay. If you prefer a more relaxed experience, the beach is a great place to sunbathe and enjoy a picnic while watching the boats and yachts that frequent the harbor.

Bonne Nuit Bay is also home to a small fishing harbor, where visitors can see traditional Jersey fishing boats. Nearby, there are cafés and restaurants where you can enjoy fresh seafood and local dishes. The bay is a lovely spot for a leisurely meal or a coffee while taking in the peaceful surroundings. A typical visit to Bonne Nuit Bay takes around 1.5 to 2 hours, but visitors who enjoy walking or photography may choose to spend more time exploring the coastal paths and enjoying the natural scenery. With its relaxed atmosphere and scenic beauty, Bonne Nuit Bay is a must-visit destination for anyone looking to experience the quieter side of Jersey.

20. Devil's Hole

Devil's Hole, located on the south coast of Jersey, is a unique natural attraction offering visitors a fascinating glimpse into the island's rugged coastline. This remarkable geological feature is a large sinkhole, formed by centuries of erosion, and it sits amidst dramatic cliffs and wild, rocky terrain. The site is renowned for its dramatic beauty and is a popular spot for those who enjoy outdoor exploration and stunning coastal views. The area surrounding Devil's Hole is also rich in local folklore, with the name of the hole itself originating from stories of it being a mysterious and dangerous place.

To get to Devil's Hole, it is approximately a 20-minute drive from St. Helier. The site is located near the La Corbière lighthouse and is accessible by foot from the nearby parking area. There is a designated parking lot where visitors can leave their cars, and from there, it's a short walk down a path to the site. The area is not serviced by public transport, so driving is the most convenient way to reach Devil's Hole. Visitors should be aware that the walk to the hole involves uneven terrain, so sturdy footwear is recommended.

There is no entry fee to visit Devil's Hole, making it an easy and free destination for tourists. The hole itself is a deep cavern in the cliffs, and during high tide, the surrounding waters create an impressive sight as they crash into the rocks below. While the hole itself is not accessible for exploration, the surrounding area offers excellent opportunities for photography, as the rugged landscape and sea views are spectacular. The site is particularly popular for those who enjoy coastal walks, as it's part of a larger network of scenic trails along the cliffs.

A visit to Devil's Hole typically takes around 30 minutes to an hour, depending on how much time you spend exploring the surrounding area and taking in the views. If you enjoy hiking, the coastal path around the area offers an additional 1-2 hours of scenic walking, with opportunities to discover other nearby viewpoints. For a peaceful and less touristy experience, Devil's Hole provides a quiet and captivating spot to enjoy the natural beauty of Jersey. Whether you are seeking a short visit or an afternoon of exploration, Devil's Hole offers an unforgettable opportunity to connect with the island's striking natural landscape.

21. The Eric Young Orchid Foundation

The Eric Young Orchid Foundation, located in the parish of Trinity on Jersey, is a renowned botanical garden dedicated to the conservation and display of orchids. Established in 1992, it has become a premier destination for orchid enthusiasts and nature lovers. The foundation is home to one of the largest collections of orchids in Europe, showcasing an impressive range of species from around the world. It serves not only as a place to admire these beautiful flowers but also as an educational facility focused on orchid conservation and cultivation.

To get to the Eric Young Orchid Foundation, it's about a 15-minute drive from St. Helier. The site is easily accessible by car, with parking available on-site for visitors. There is also a bus route that connects St. Helier to the area, with a short walk to the foundation from the nearest stop. For those looking to explore Jersey's natural beauty, the foundation is located near several scenic walking paths, providing the opportunity to enjoy the island's landscape on the way.

The entry fee to the Eric Young Orchid Foundation is generally around £7 for adults and £3 for children. It is advisable to check the website or call ahead for specific pricing and opening hours, as these may vary depending on the season. The foundation is typically open from April to October, though it may offer special events or seasonal openings during the rest of the year. Visitors to the foundation can explore its extensive collection of orchids, which are displayed in purpose-built glasshouses and gardens. The orchid collection is diverse, including both tropical and temperate species, as well as rare and endangered varieties. The foundation is committed to orchid conservation, and guests can learn about the ongoing research and efforts to protect these delicate plants. In addition to the orchid displays, there are educational exhibits that explain the importance of orchid conservation and the challenges facing these unique plants in the wild.

A visit to the Eric Young Orchid Foundation typically takes between 1 to 1.5 hours, depending on your level of interest in the exhibits and gardens. The site is peaceful and offers an excellent opportunity to relax while admiring the stunning variety of orchids. There is also a small gift shop where visitors can purchase orchid-related products and souvenirs. Whether you're an orchid enthusiast or simply appreciate beautiful gardens, the Eric Young Orchid Foundation provides an educational and visually captivating experience.

When visiting Jersey here are 7 valuable pieces of advice to keep in mind:

1. Always check the weather before heading out. Jersey's weather can be unpredictable, especially near the coast, so it's best to pack layers and bring a waterproof jacket. Be prepared for sudden changes in conditions, particularly if you plan on walking or hiking in the more rugged parts of the island.

2. Consider renting a car or using public transport to explore the island. While Jersey has a good bus service, renting a car offers more flexibility, especially if you plan on visiting remote beaches or countryside areas. Parking is generally not an issue in most places, but it can get busy during peak tourist season, so plan ahead.

3. Bring comfortable footwear. Jersey is known for its beautiful coastal walks and scenic trails, many of which involve uneven terrain. Whether you're heading to St. Brelade's Bay or hiking around the cliffs near La Corbière, sturdy shoes will make the experience much more enjoyable.

4. Be mindful of the island's rich history and culture. Jersey has a fascinating mix of French and British influences, and it's important to respect local customs and traditions. When visiting sites like Mont Orgueil Castle or the Jersey War Tunnels, take time to learn about the island's wartime history and its heritage.

5. Jersey is famous for its fresh seafood, so be sure to try local delicacies like lobster, crab, or the traditional Jersey Royals potatoes. Many coastal cafés and restaurants offer delicious dishes made from locally sourced ingredients.

6. Make sure to bring sunscreen and a hat, especially during the summer months. Despite being located in the Channel, Jersey enjoys a relatively mild climate, but the sun can still be intense on the island's beaches, so protecting your skin is important.

7. Lastly, remember that Jersey operates on British Summer Time (BST) during the summer months, so adjust your schedule accordingly, particularly if you are coming from another time zone. This will help you make the most of your day trips and sightseeing.

Here are 7 of the best services to consider using:

1. Jersey's public transportation system is an efficient and convenient way to get around the island. The bus service operates regularly, covering most major towns, beaches, and attractions. It's an affordable option, especially if you don't want to rent a car, and it's eco-friendly, too. Buses are well-maintained and provide a stress-free way to explore Jersey without the hassle of parking.

2. For those looking to explore more remote areas, bike rentals are an excellent service to consider. Jersey has a number of cycling routes that take you through beautiful countryside and along the coast. Several local businesses offer bike rentals, providing you with an affordable way to enjoy the island's natural beauty at your own pace.

3. If you prefer the convenience of a guided tour, booking a local tour guide can enrich your visit. Knowledgeable guides can offer insights into Jersey's history, culture, and wildlife. Whether you're interested in island history, hiking tours, or discovering hidden gems, local tour operators can craft an itinerary tailored to your interests.

4. When it comes to accommodation, Jersey offers a variety of options, from charming boutique hotels to luxurious seaside resorts. Services like booking websites can help you find the best deals and make reservations easily.

5. For food lovers, Jersey's farmers' markets are a must-visit. Local markets, such as the one in St. Helier, provide fresh, locally sourced produce and artisanal products. Shopping here supports local farmers and provides an authentic taste of Jersey's produce, including the famous Jersey Royals potatoes.

6. If you're interested in exploring the island by sea, consider using boat tours or charter services. You can explore Jersey's coastline, visit nearby islands, or even go whale watching. These services offer a unique perspective of the island and provide unforgettable views of the sea and surrounding landscape.

7. Lastly, consider using local concierge services for personalized assistance during your stay. These services can help with everything from booking reservations at top restaurants to arranging transportation or planning special activities.

Top 7 Must-Try Dining Spots in Jersey:

1. The Royal Yacht Hotel's Grill – Located in St. Helier, this modern and stylish restaurant is renowned for its fresh seafood and exceptional service. Enjoy panoramic views of St. Aubin's Bay while dining on a selection of locally caught fish, grilled meats, and delicious desserts.

2. La Mare Vineyards – For a unique dining experience, head to La Mare Vineyards, where you can enjoy a meal paired with wines produced right on the premises. The vineyard's restaurant serves dishes made with local ingredients, and you can also tour the vineyard and sample its wines.

3. The Harbour Gallery Café – Situated near St. Aubin, this charming café offers a cozy atmosphere and delicious homemade cakes, light meals, and fresh coffee. It's a perfect spot to relax after exploring the local art gallery, where you can view works from local artists.

4. Sirocco – Known for its fine dining, Sirocco is an elegant restaurant offering a modern menu with a focus on seafood and international flavors. Located on the waterfront in St. Helier, Sirocco offers diners a memorable experience with its contemporary décor and exceptional dishes.

5. Bohemia Restaurant – As one of Jersey's most acclaimed restaurants, Bohemia in St. Helier offers a Michelin-star dining experience. The restaurant is known for its inventive approach to modern British cuisine, combining local ingredients with unique international twists.

6. The Crab Shack – Situated on St. Brelade's Bay, this casual beachfront spot serves some of the island's freshest lobster and seafood in a relaxed setting. Perfect for enjoying a light, fresh meal while overlooking the beautiful bay.

7. The Salty Dog – Located in St. Aubin, The Salty Dog is a lively pub offering delicious locally sourced food and craft beers. It's a great place for a relaxed meal, with options ranging from fresh seafood to hearty pub classics.

Here are 7 crucial phone numbers to know:

1. Emergency Services – For any emergency, whether it's fire, police, or medical, dial 112 or 999. Both numbers connect you to the appropriate emergency services on the island. It's always a good idea to have this number memorized in case of an urgent situation.

2. Police Non-Emergency – For non-urgent police matters, such as reporting a crime or seeking advice, you can call 01534 612612. This number is available for less critical issues where immediate response isn't required.

3. Jersey General Hospital – If you need medical attention or advice, you can contact the Jersey General Hospital at 01534 442000. The hospital provides emergency care and general health services for both residents and tourists.

4. St. Helier Tourist Information – For any inquiries regarding local attractions, tours, or services, you can reach the St. Helier Tourist Information Centre at 01534 500444. The center is a great resource for maps, guides, and advice on things to do around the island.

5. Jersey Taxi Service – If you need transportation around the island, Jersey's taxi service can be reached at 01534 700700. Taxis are available throughout Jersey, offering a convenient way to travel without the need for a car rental.

6. Jersey Water – For any water-related issues or inquiries, such as disruptions in supply or reporting leaks, you can contact Jersey Water at 01534 707300. The company provides clean, safe drinking water for the island's residents and visitors.

7. Jersey Post – For postal services or tracking deliveries, Jersey Post can be contacted at 01534 616616. Whether you need to send postcards, packages, or get postal rates, this number will connect you with the island's postal services.

7 unknown facts about Jersey:

1. Jersey has its own currency. While the island uses British pounds, it also issues its own currency, known as the Jersey pound. This currency is pegged to the British pound and can be used interchangeably, but it's not legal tender in the UK.

2. The island has a long history of cheese production. Jersey is renowned for its dairy farming, particularly the Jersey cow breed, which is famous for its rich milk. The island has been producing its own distinctive cheeses for centuries, including the well-known Jersey Blue and its cream-based products.

3. The island was once a German military stronghold. During World War II, Jersey was occupied by German forces for five years. Many remnants of this period remain, including bunkers, tunnels, and fortifications, which can be explored at sites like the Jersey War Tunnels and Battery Lothringen.

4. Jersey has its own legal system. Although the island is a British Crown Dependency, it operates under its own legal framework, distinct from that of the UK. Jersey's laws are influenced by both Norman law and its unique governance, which allows it a degree of autonomy.

5. The island is home to one of Europe's oldest working lighthouses. The Corbière Lighthouse, built in 1874, stands at the southwestern tip of the island and is still in operation today. It has become an iconic symbol of Jersey's rugged coastline.

6. Jersey has a unique climate. The island enjoys a mild climate thanks to the Gulf Stream, making it one of the warmest places in the UK. It has more sunshine hours than many parts of the British Isles and is ideal for growing subtropical plants like palms and agapanthus.

7. The island has a strong maritime heritage. Jersey has been a key player in maritime trade for centuries, and its harbors remain bustling with activity. The island was once known for its shipbuilding industry, and you can explore its maritime history at the Maritime Museum in St. Helier.

Printed in Dunstable, United Kingdom

74210508R00016